MIGHTY MILITARY MACHINES

Military Drones

by Matt Scheff

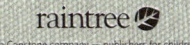

a Capstone company — publishers for children

Raintree is an imprint of Capstone Global Library Limited, a company incorporated in England and Wales having its registered office at 264 Banbury Road, Oxford, OX2 7DY – Registered company number: 6695582

www.raintree.co.uk
myorders@raintree.co.uk

Text © Capstone Global Library Limited 2019
The moral rights of the proprietor have been asserted.

All rights reserved. No part of this publication may be reproduced in any form or by any means (including photocopying or storing it in any medium by electronic means and whether or not transiently or incidentally to some other use of this publication) without the written permission of the copyright owner, except in accordance with the provisions of the Copyright, Designs and Patents Act 1988 or under the terms of a licence issued by the Copyright Licensing Agency, Barnard's Inn, 86 Fetter Lane, London, EC4A 1EN (www.cla.co.uk). Applications for the copyright owner's written permission should be addressed to the publisher.

Edited by Marissa Kirkman
Designed by Heidi Thompson
Picture research by Jo Miller
Production by Tori Abraham
Originated by Capstone Global Library Ltd
Printed and bound in India

ISBN 978 1 4747 6173 4
22 21 20 19 18
10 9 8 7 6 5 4 3 2 1

British Library Cataloguing in Publication Data
A full catalogue record for this book is available from the British Library.

Acknowledgements
We would like to thank the following for permission to reproduce photographs:
Air National Guard photo by Senior Airman Michael Quiboloy, 9, Tech. Sgt. Neil Ballecer, 19; U.S. Air Force photo by Airman 1st Class Aaron Montoya, 12, 17, Master Sgt. Robert W. Valenca, 5, Master Sgt. Steve Horton, 13, Tech Sgt. Effrain Lopez, cover, Tech. Sgt. Kevin J. Gruenwald, 11; Visual Information Specialist Paolo Bovo, 7; U.S. Navy: Photo courtesy of Northrop Grumman, 15; Wikimedia: U.S. Air Force photo, 21

Design elements: Shutterstock: Zerbor

Every effort has been made to contact copyright holders of material reproduced in this book. Any omissions will be rectified in subsequent printings if notice is given to the publisher.

All the internet addresses (URLs) given in this book were valid at the time of going to press. However, due to the dynamic nature of the internet, some addresses may have changed, or sites may have changed or ceased to exist since publication. While the author and publisher regret any inconvenience this may cause readers, no responsibility for any such changes can be accepted by either the author or the publisher.

Contents

Drones 4

Take off 8

Parts of a drone 12

    Glossary 22
    Read more 23
    Website 23
    Comprehension questions 24
    Index 24

Drones

What is that in the sky? It is a military drone. Some drones look like planes but they are not planes.

Drones are flying machines.
Some drones are large and look like real planes.
Other drones are small and look a bit like model planes.

Take off

A drone speeds along a runway.

It is very fast.

The drone takes off!

The pilots do not sit inside the drone.
They fly the drone from a control room.
The pilots use computers to help them fly the drone.

Parts of a drone

Drones carry cameras. They can spy. The drones take photos from the air.

camera

Some military drones can shoot weapons. Pilots use computers to fire weapons from the control room.

This is the engine of a drone.

It powers the drone.

It makes it fly.

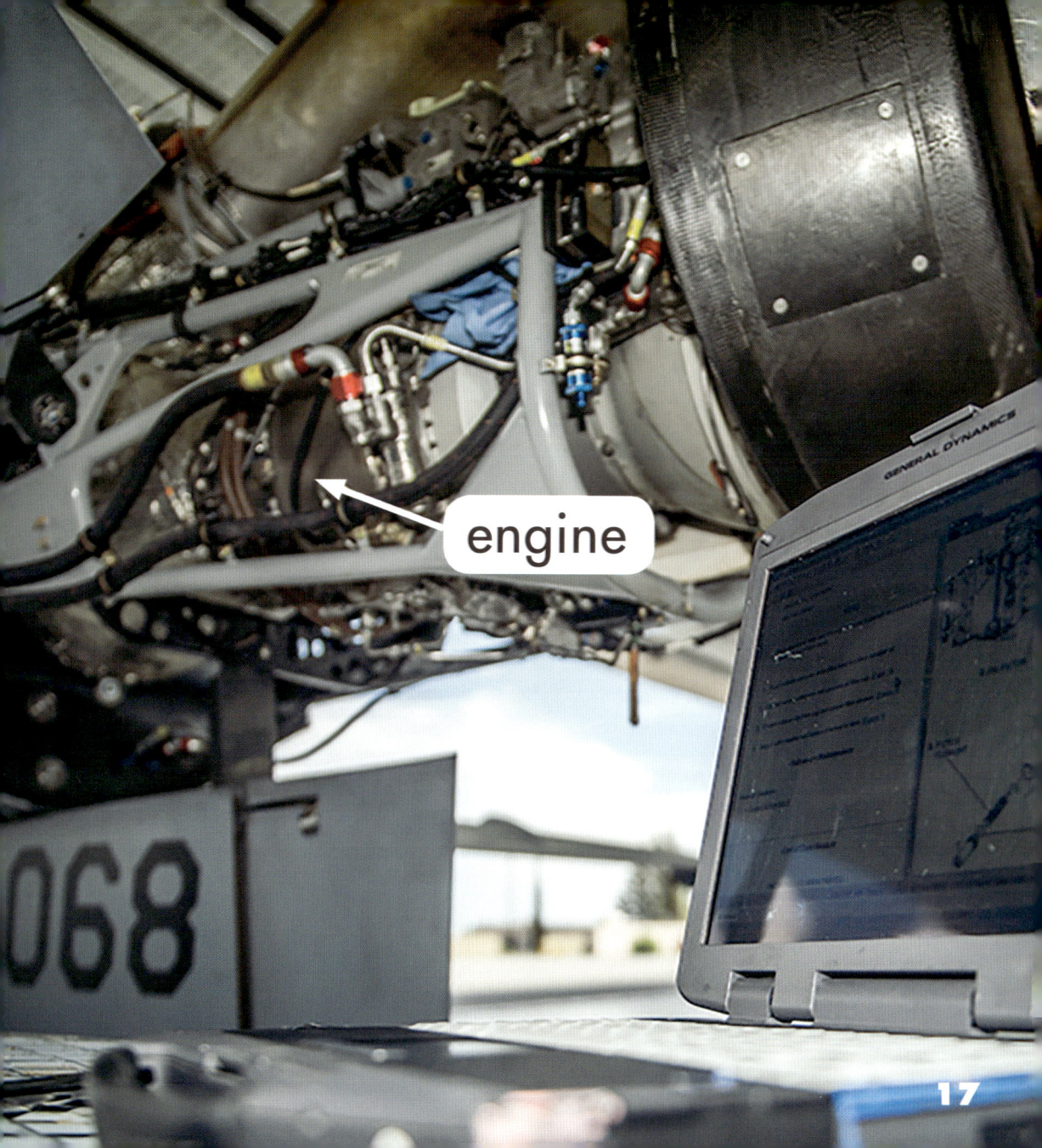

The wings lift the drone. It flies high and far. The drone has wheels. The wheels roll along the runway when the drone takes off and lands.

Military drones are used in battles. The pilots are safe. They are far away in the control room and not in the drone.

Glossary

control room room with equipment used to command machines that are far away

engine machine that makes the power needed to move something or make it work

military to do with the armed forces such as the army or the air force

pilot person who flies a jet or plane

runway area or strip of land where planes take off and land

spy secretly collect information about an enemy

weapon something used to harm an enemy in a battle or fight

wings parts of a plane on each side of the aircraft that make it able to fly

Read more

Drones (Usborne Beginners Plus), Henry Brook (Usborne Publishing Ltd, 2016)

Military Drones (Drones), Matt Chandler (Raintree, 2018)

Robots (DKfindout!), Dr Nathan Lepora (DK Children, 2018)

Website

Find out more about military aircraft at: www.dkfindout.com/uk/transport/history-aircraft/military-aircraft

Comprehension questions

1. Who flies a drone?
2. What do drones do when they are spying?
3. Which part gives a drone its power?

Index

control rooms 10, 14
engines 16
flying 6, 10, 18
photos 12
pilots 10, 20
shooting 14
spying 12
taking off 8
weapons 14
wings 18